Money Around the World

What Is Money?

Rebecca Rissman

Heinemann Library
Chicago, Illinois

Customer Service 888-454-2279
Visit our website at www.heinemannraintree.com

Designed by Joanna Hinton-Malivoire
Photo Research by Tracy Cummins and Heather Mauldin
Printed and bound in the United States of America, North Mankato, MN

15 14 13
10 9 8 7 6 5

The Library of Congress has cataloged the first edition as follows:
Rissman, Rebecca.
   What is money? / Rebecca Rissman.
      p. cm. -- (Money around the world)
   Includes bibliographical references and index.
   ISBN 978-1-4329-1072-3 (hc) -- ISBN 978-1-4329-1077-8 (pb) 1. Money--Juvenile literature. I. Title.
   HG221.5.R57 2008
   332.4--dc22
                                        2007035535
   052013
   007415R

Acknowledgments
The author and publisher are grateful to the following for permission to reproduce copyright material: ©Getty Images pp. **4**, **23a** (Chien-min Chung), **5**, **23b** (Cosmo Condina), **6** (AFP/ATTA KENARE), **8** (Oliver Benn), **9** (AFP/KAZUHIRO NOGI), **10** (Darren Robb), **13** (Olaf Tiedje), **14** (Gary John Norman), **15** (Andrew Hetherington), **16** (Keith Brofsky), **17** (Stephen Derr), **18** (AFP/KIM JAE-HWAN), **19** (Altrendo Images), **20** (Lorne Resnick), **21** (Absodels); ©istockphoto pp. **11** (ILYA GENKIN), **12** (Sean Lock); ©Masterfile p. **22** (Royalty Free); ©The World Bank p. **7** (Curt Carnemark).

Cover photograph reproduced with permission of ©istockphoto (ILYA GENKIN).
Back cover photograph reproduced with the permission of Getty Images (Gary John Norman).

Every effort has been made to contact copyright holders of any material reproduced in this book. Any omissions will be rectified in subsequent printings if notice is given to the publisher.

Contents

What Is Money?

People use money to buy things.

People use money to trade.

taxi driver

People trade work for money.

People trade things for money.

People trade money for things
they want.

People trade money for things
they need.

Types of Money

Coins are money.

Bills are money.

Checks are money.

Credit cards are money.

Using Money

People trade coins to buy things.

People trade bills to buy things.

People trade checks to buy things.

People use credit cards to buy things.

Some things cost a little money.

Some things cost a lot of money.

Money Around the World

People trade with each other around the world.

People use money around the world.

Different Kinds of Money

Money looks different around the world.

Picture Glossary

 **money** something traded for work or things. Money can be bills, coins, checks or credit cards.

 **trade** to give something in order to receive something else

Index

Note to Parents and Teachers

Before reading: Ask children to tell you what they already know about money. Do they know what money looks like? Can they name different kinds of money?

After reading: Discuss with children that money is what people use to trade for goods or services. Then, turn to the image on page 11. This image shows many different kinds of currency used around the world. Use this image to prompt discussion about the many different countries shown throughout the book.